The Story of the Atomic Bomb

How It Changed the World

The World Transformed

BY NATALIE M. ROSINSKY

Content Adviser:
Peter Barker, Ph.D., Professor,
Department of the History of Science,
University of Oklahoma

Reading Adviser:
Alexa L. Sandmann, Ed.D., Professor of Literacy,
College and Graduate School of Education, Health, and
Human Services, Kent State University

Compass Point Books
151 Good Counsel Drive
P.O. Box 669
Mankato, MN 56002-0669

Editor: Jennifer Fretland VanVoorst
Designer: Ashlee Suker
Media Researcher: Eric Gohl
Library Consultant: Kathleen Baxter
Production Specialist: Jane Klenk

Image Credits: DVIC/NARA, 35; Getty Images Inc./AFP, 38, 46; Getty
Images Inc./AFP/William West, 57; Getty Images Inc./Embassy Pictures,
51; Getty Images Inc./Hulton Archive, 42; Getty Images Inc./Joe Raedle, 7;
Getty Images Inc./Keystone, 26; Getty Images Inc./Liaison/Brad Markel,
53; Getty Images Inc./MPI, 16, 36; Getty Images Inc./Photographer's
Choice/Michael Dunning, 52; Getty Images Inc./Picture Post, 29; Getty
Images Inc./Time Life Pictures/Alfred Eisenstaedt, 21; Getty Images Inc./
Time Life Pictures/Bernard Hoffman, 13, 37; Getty Images Inc./Time Life
Pictures/Ed Clark, 24; Getty Images Inc./Time Life Pictures/Los Alamos
National Laboratory, 31; Getty Images Inc./Time Life Pictures/Marie
Hansen, 19; Library of Congress, 5, 8, 12, 17, 28, 34, 41, 47, 50; National
Archives and Records Administration, 11, 32; Newscom/AFP Photo, 55;
Wikipedia, public-domain image, 1, 45, cover.

Library of Congress Cataloging-in-Publication Data
Rosinsky, Natalie M. (Natalie Myra)
  The story of the atomic bomb : how it changed the world / by Natalie
M. Rosinsky.
    p. cm. — (The world transformed)
  Includes bibliographical references and index.
  ISBN 978-0-7565-4316-7 (library binding)
  1. Atomic bomb—History—Juvenile literature. 2. Nuclear
energy—History—Juvenile literature. I. Title. II. Series.
  QC773.A1R67 2010
  355.02'17—dc22   2009034869

Visit Compass Point Books on the Internet at *www.compasspointbooks.com*
or e-mail your request to *custserv@compasspointbooks.com*

TABLE OF CONTENTS

□ Chapter 1

OPERATION TRINITY

J ust before dawn on July 16, 1945, a secret U.S. project changed the world forever. In New Mexico, scientists and soldiers watched with awe the explosion of a new invention, an atomic bomb. The blast—as strong as 20,000 tons (18,000 metric tons) of TNT—astonished its creators, even though they had planned for it. Physicist Isidor Rabi later described the atom bomb test, code-named Operation Trinity:

Suddenly there was an enormous flash of light, the brightest light I have ever seen or that I think anyone has ever seen. It blasted; it pounced; it bored its way right through you. It was a vision which was seen with more than the eye. It seemed to last forever. You would wish it to stop; altogether it lasted two seconds. Finally it was over ... [and] where the bomb had been, there was an enormous ball of fire which grew and grew and it rolled as it grew; it went up into the air, in yellow flashes and into scarlet and green. It looked menacing. It seemed to come towards one.

The mushroom cloud generated by the first atomic bomb was photographed from six miles (9.6 kilometers) away.

A tower of black dust and smoke trailed the fireball. The tower rose so quickly that in seconds it was taller than the Empire State Building. A few minutes later the mushrooming cloud was eight miles (13 kilometers) high.

The heat of the blast also shocked some observers. One scientist expected the blinding light but not the "blinding heat." Even 10 miles (16 km) away, he said, "It was like opening a hot oven with the sun coming out like a sunrise." Actually 10,000 times as hot as the sun's surface, the explosion

MAKING AND RECORDING HISTORY

Many of the people who developed the atom bomb had strong opinions about the extraordinary weapon. Their letters, diaries, interviews with reporters, and autobiographies have become part of history. From these unofficial accounts, we know that one man witnessing the Trinity explosion exclaimed, "My God, it's beautiful." "No," his companion replied, "it's terrible."

A famous quotation summed up the opposing views of the atom bomb. J. Robert Oppenheimer, the head U.S. scientist on the secret project, had studied sacred Hindu writings. As he watched the Trinity explosion, Oppenheimer voiced both awe and regret at his triumph. He quoted an ancient Hindu poem:

If the radiance of a thousand suns
Were to burst at once into the sky,
That would be like the splendor
Of the Mighty One ...
I am become Death, the Destroyer of worlds.

melted the desert sand into a green glassy substance. This was later named trinitite, for Operation Trinity. The thundering roar that followed the explosion impressed other observers. A soldier miles away said the blast sounded like an anti-aircraft cannon just yards away. A scientist compared the blast's roar to the sound of an express train passing within inches.

The force and heat of the Trinity explosion destroyed all plants and wildlife within a mile (1.6 km) of the blast. Its

Trinitite still can be found at the test site; it is radioactive and requires careful handling.

shock waves threw some standing observers to the ground and broke windows in towns 120 miles (192 km) away. Unaware of the secret project, some people in these communities thought an earthquake had occurred. Others thought an airplane or a meteor had crashed. Eight-year-old Thomas Treat of Deming, New Mexico, thought the world might be ending. He had been sleeping on his family's front porch when the explosion's startling light woke him and the family roosters.

Some people near the test site believed the United States had been attacked. Their fears, while wrong, were closer to the truth. The atom bomb had been invented as a weapon—more

J. Robert Oppenheimer and General Leslie R. Groves, leaders of the secret project, examined the remains of a tower destroyed by the bomb.

destructive than any created before. The United States was at war. Its leaders were in a desperate race to develop the atomic bomb before its enemies could develop this incredibly powerful weapon themselves.

HIDING THE TRUTH

Government officials explained Operation Trinity's blast with a lie. The Associated Press reported this supposed "news" in a brief article:

ALAMORGORDO, JULY 16—The Commanding Officer of the Alamogordo Army Air Force Base made the following statement today: "Several inquiries have been received concerning a certain heavy explosion which occurred on the Alamogordo Base reservation this morning. A remotely located ammunition magazine containing a considerable amount of high explosives and pyrotechnics exploded. There was no loss of life or injury to anyone, and the property damage outside of the explosives maga-zine itself was negligible. Weather conditions affecting the content of gas shells exploded by the blast may make it desirable for the Army to evacuate temporarily a few civilians from their homes."

Chapter 2

A WORLD AT WAR

The conflicts of World War II (1939–1945) simmered and erupted long before the United States entered the war in 1941. In Europe problems began in 1933, when Adolf Hitler became chancellor of Germany. He and his followers, called Nazis, imposed harsh regulations and racist laws that stripped Jews and other minority groups of their rights. If non-Jews protested this unfairness, they, like the Jews, risked losing their jobs, their property, their freedom, and even their lives.

Hitler wanted Germany to conquer Europe, and the Germans started World War II in September 1939 by invading Poland. By the middle of 1940, Germany controlled most of Europe. Nazi officials were brutal and violent. They devised a system called the "Final Solution" to kill all Jews. It included prisons called concentration camps. Before the Nazis were defeated in 1945, they had massacred more than 6 million Jews and millions of other people from Germany and the conquered countries.

Starving prisoners at Buchenwald, one of the largest of Germany's concentration camps

Nazi policies played an important role in the story of the atom bomb. Since the early 1900s, German universities had been centers of scientific research. Many breakthroughs in understanding atoms—tiny particles of matter—were made by German scientists or others who studied or worked with them. When Hitler came to power, nearly 400 German scientists fled to escape Nazi policies. Some of these brilliant people were Jews or had Jewish relatives. Others simply could not stand living and working under Nazi rule.

The most famous of the refugees was Albert Einstein.

The German-Jewish physicist had won the Nobel Prize in 1921. His theory about the relationship between matter and energy, summed up in the equation $E = mc^2$, proved that matter could become energy. This theory brought him worldwide renown. Einstein settled in the United States, working at Princeton University.

Other physicists whose research directly involved atoms also fled to the United States. These included Hungarian

Albert Einstein is considered by many to be the founder of modern physics and the greatest scientist of the 20th century.

Jews Leo Szilard and Edward Teller, German Hans Bethe, and Italian Enrico Fermi, whose wife was Jewish. (Italy's leader, Benito Mussolini, was an ally of Hitler.) Danish physicist Niels Bohr reached the United States later.

As early as 1933, Leo Szilard imagined that splitting one atom might somehow split other atoms, in a process called a chain reaction. Each atom would release energy when it split. A chain reaction might release so much energy that it would cause an explosion. Physicist Lise Meitner was an Austrian Jew who found shelter in Sweden. There, in 1938, she suggested that atomic experiments by German scientists actually showed atoms splitting, a process called fission. Atomic fission suggested a practical way to start a chain reaction for the first time. These ideas

A scientist worked with an atom smasher used for atomic fission in 1941.

FROM SCIENCE FICTION TO SCIENCE FACT

There is often a connection between scientific discoveries and science fiction. Leo Szilard and other inventors of the atom bomb were familiar with H.G. Wells' 1914 novel about the future, *The World Set Free*. In the book, scientists discover a way to harness atomic power and create atom bombs:

> [N]ot only should we have a source of power so potent that a man might carry in his hand the energy to light a city for a year, fight a fleet of battleships, or drive one of our giant ships across the Atlantic; but we should also have a clue that ... would mean a change in human conditions. ... [W]ith both hands, the bomb-thrower lifted the big atom bomb ... The bomb flashed blinding scarlet in mid-air, and fell, a descending column of blaze ... in the middle of a whirlwind ... and a third column of fire rushed eddying down upon the doomed buildings below.

Wells probably drew upon earlier scientific investigations of the atom. In 1897 English physicist Joseph Thomson had discovered electrons, one kind of particle inside an atom. New Zealand physicist Ernest Rutherford studied radioactive elements. In 1911 he announced the discovery of the atom's dense core—the nucleus. In 1913 Niels Bohr took Rutherford's work further, explaining how electrons give off energy.

became the basis of the first working atom bombs.

These refugee physicists knew that German scientists were continuing to study atomic fission. Fearing what the Nazis might do with an atom bomb, Szilard and others wanted to warn President Franklin D. Roosevelt. They felt the United States should begin its own atomic research program. But would Roosevelt listen to them? In the summer of 1939, Szilard enlisted the help of the world's most famous scientist—Albert Einstein—to explain the dangers.

After speaking at length with Szilard and Eugene Wigner, another refugee physicist, Einstein wrote to President Roosevelt on August 2, 1939. In part, his letter said:

> [I]t may become possible to set up a nuclear chain reaction in a large mass of uranium by which vast amounts of power ... would be generated. Now it appears almost certain that this could be achieved in the immediate future.
>
> This phenomenon would also lead to the construction of bombs, and it is conceivable ... that extremely powerful bombs of a new type may thus be constructed. A single bomb of this type, carried by boat and exploded in a port, might very well destroy the whole port together with some of the surrounding territory. ...
>
> In view of this situation you may think it desirable to have some permanent contact maintained between the

Administration and the group of physicists working on chain reactions in America … to speed up the experimental work, which at present is being carried out within the limits of budgets of University laboratories … and perhaps also by obtaining the co-operation of industrial laboratories which have the necessary equipment. …

Very truly yours,

Albert Einstein

Albert Einstein
Old Grove Rd.
Nassau Point
Peconic, Long Island

August 2nd, 1939

F.D. Roosevelt,
President of the United States,
White House
Washington, D.C.

Sir:

Some recent work by E.Fermi and L. Szilard, which has been communicated to me in manuscript, leads me to expect that the element uranium may be turned into a new and important source of energy in the immediate future. Certain aspects of the situation which has arisen seem to call for watchfulness and, if necessary, quick action on the part of the Administration. I believe therefore that it is my duty to bring to your attention the following facts and recommendations:

In the course of the last four months it has been made probable - through the work of Joliot in France as well as Fermi and Szilard in America - that it may become possible to set up a nuclear chain reaction in a large mass of uranium,by which vast amounts of power and large quantities of new radium-like elements would be generated. Now it appears almost certain that this could be achieved in the immediate future.

This new phenomenon would also lead to the construction of bombs, and it is conceivable - though much less certain - that extremely powerful bombs of a new type may thus be constructed. A single bomb of this type, carried by boat and exploded in a port, might very well destroy the whole port together with some of the surrounding territory. However, such bombs might very well prove to be too heavy for transportation by air.

Einstein's letter to President Roosevelt is regarded as the start of the atomic bomb project.

Roosevelt took Einstein's advice. He created an official committee, including Army and Navy representatives, to investigate the uranium research Einstein had mentioned.

Thanks to refugee scientists, the U.S. government knew about atom bombs before it was drawn into World War II on December 7, 1941. A sneak attack on the Navy base at Pearl

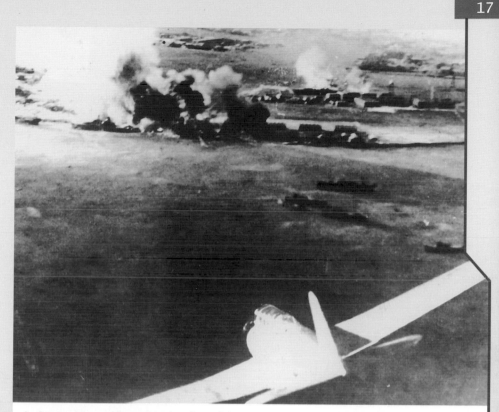

∧ Japanese pilot beginning his attack photographed the destruction at Hawaii's Pearl Harbor.

Harbor, Hawaii, by the Japanese—Hitler's allies—caused the U.S. to declare war on Japan, Germany, and Italy.

The Japanese had used conventional bombs and other weapons at Pearl Harbor—like the ones used in their earlier attacks on Manchuria and China. Germany also had not yet used atom bombs in its European conquests or raids on England. Yet Roosevelt feared that atom bombs might soon be part of Germany's arsenal. The United States had to develop its own atomic weapons first. The race was on, and the country's safety and freedom were at stake.

—□ Chapter **3**

THE MANHATTAN PROJECT

The United States had to speed up and coordinate its research on splitting atoms. No scientist had yet achieved a safe, working chain reaction to prove that the theory behind atom bombs held true. Once that was accomplished, the bomb itself would have to be designed, built, and tested.

To manage all these challenges, President Roosevelt's advisers appointed a veteran Army engineer—General Leslie R. Groves. This blunt, short-tempered man had recently supervised construction of the huge Pentagon building, the new headquarters for the U.S. military. Groves took charge of the secret Manhattan Project (named for the borough of New York City where many of its early operations were conducted) in June 1942. He soon decided to build two kinds of bomb: one using the element uranium, and one using the element plutonium.

Groves began gathering his team. One obstacle he faced was the distrust some scientists felt toward the military.

Another was the commitment of time and effort being asked of scientists. British researchers had estimated that it would take two to three years to produce an atom bomb. Groves started by choosing J. Robert Oppenheimer to be the project's head scientist.

Oppenheimer was a brilliant physicist with a magnetic personality. He persuaded many scientists to join the Manhattan Project. In the next few months, this rail-thin, intense man drew U. S. scientists as well as refugees into the project.

General Leslie R. Groves' choice of J. Robert Oppenheimer (right) helped to recruit other top scientists for the Manhattan Project.

"THE ITALIAN NAVIGATOR HAS LANDED"

On December 2, 1942, a mysterious phone conversation took place. From the University of Chicago, physicist Arthur Holly Compton spoke to an adviser of President Roosevelt. Compton had exciting news to share about the secret Manhattan Project. He spoke in code as he said:

> [T]he Italian navigator has landed in the new world. ... The earth was not as large as he had estimated, and he arrived at the new world sooner than he had expected. ... Everyone landed safe and happy.

The "Italian navigator" in this message was physicist Enrico Fermi, who had just successfully produced the first atomic chain reaction. This was the "new world" that he—like Christopher Columbus landing in America—had reached.

Working in a hidden university laboratory, Fermi and his team had built the world's first nuclear reactor. This "pile," as they called it, caused uranium atoms to split. The resulting chain reaction was controlled by cadmium rods. Some people had wondered whether a chain reaction could be stopped before it caused an explosion. That is why Compton reassured his listener that "Everyone landed safe and happy." The work of building an atom bomb could now begin.

California's Ernest Lawrence and Glenn Seaborg—along with refugees Edward Teller, Leo Szilard, and Enrico Fermi—were among the first to join. Young Richard Feynman from Princeton University and Leona Woods from the University of Chicago were among those who soon followed.

At first Oppenheimer thought he would need 30 to 100 scientists to build an atom bomb. As the Manhattan Project developed, though, its staff increased to more than 4,000 civilians and 2,000 military specialists. There were also thousands of support workers, including builders, cooks, and cleaners. Many people who joined the project did not

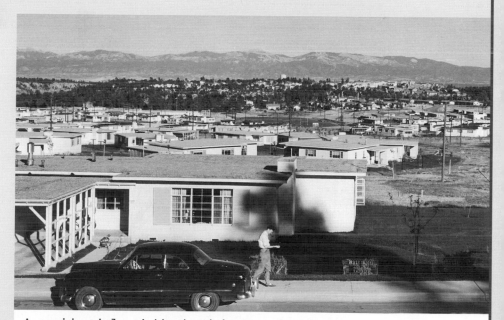

A residential neighborhood in Los Alamos, New Mexico, housed workers on the top-secret Manhattan Project.

know where they would be living. When they reached their destination, they could not tell anyone where they were. The nature and location of the Manhattan Project were kept top secret to prevent the country's enemies from finding out about it.

The project eventually had three secret locations. Each grew to be a small city. Each was selected to play a certain role in developing the atom bomb. Los Alamos, New Mexico, became the first, central site in April 1943. Its location, on a mesa, was where the bombs would be built. Roads and railroads were near enough to bring in supplies, and few people lived within 100 miles (161 km). This helped to keep the project secret. Oppenheimer was also pleased by this choice because he had spent many vacations in the New Mexico desert. He once wrote, "My two great loves are physics and desert country." Now his wish to combine these two loves had come true.

Project workers referred to Los Alamos as Site Y or just "the Hill." They nicknamed the two atom bombs they built there "Fat Man" and "Little Boy." The materials for the bombs came from Site X, in Oak Ridge, Tennessee, and Site W, in Hanford, Washington. The Oak Ridge site used hydroelectric power from nearby dams and rivers to produce the type of uranium used in the bombs. At times its four manufacturing plants used more electricity than New York City.

BEHIND THE SCENES

Many scientists, technicians, and workers brought their families to the Manhattan Project's remote sites. These secret cities included schools, churches, and community centers, as well as research buildings and manufacturing plants. Like most public places in parts of the United States then, the communities were segregated by race. African-Americans lived, worked, and played apart from whites. High-ranking scientists and military officers usually had better housing than other people in the project.

Daily life went on, yet young children and teens knew that secret, vital war work surrounded them. At Los Alamos, adults spent many hours creating something kids knew only as "the Gadget." This mysterious project had an unexpected side benefit for kids. Dana Mitchell lived at Los Alamos from age 10 to 12. He recalled:

We were always raiding the junk pile there. In the Project, they decided that it was a lot better to throw stuff out than to repair it. By the time they could have repaired something, they would have invented a better version anyway. So this junk pile filled up with discarded electronics and lab equipment. And ... we grabbed whatever we wanted and filled our bedrooms.

The Hanford site, drawing hydroelectric power from the Columbia River, produced plutonium. Mud plagued workers in rainy Hanford and damp Oak Ridge, while whirling desert dust added to the daily pressures of life in Los Alamos.

Those pressures included the high level of secrecy that General Groves demanded. Only Oppenheimer and the military commander had telephones. All mail leaving Los Alamos was opened and censored. The barbed wire that surrounded the site painfully reminded refugee scientists of

A sign at the Oak Ridge, Tennessee, facility warned workers to keep quiet about the project.

Nazi concentration camps. They had fled Europe only to find themselves in what felt like another kind of prison.

Fun-loving Richard Feynman, though, had a different response to secrecy measures such as the fence. The 24-year-old physicist teased officials about it. One day Feynman discovered a hole in the fence and used it for a practical joke. He mysteriously kept reappearing inside and then outside the barrier. He revealed his prank only after bewildered guards brought him in for questioning. Feynman's casual attitude, however, was not a typical response to the harsh regulations.

Leo Szilard, among others, believed that Groves' emphasis on secrecy added obstacles to their research. Groves insisted that scientists not discuss their progress or problems with researchers working on other parts of the bomb. Szilard disobeyed. He said science advanced through sharing ideas. Oppenheimer managed to settle this dispute just before Groves was to have Szilard arrested.

The stress-filled race to produce an atom bomb continued. In 1943 and 1944, Allied forces helped meet this challenge by destroying some German resources for bomb-making. These included a manufacturing plant in conquered Norway, where Germans were creating materials for their own bomb project. Manhattan Project experts, however, still felt that the clock was ticking. German scientists might be keeping pace or even be ahead of them.

Ernest Lawrence invented an atom smasher called the
Cyclotron. A modified design helped to make the uranium
for the Little Boy bomb.

The German bomb scientists actually were far behind the
Manhattan Project researchers. This became known in
April 1945, when U.S. forces captured Hitler's atom bomb
experts in Germany. Soon after, an unexpected tragedy
raised another, significant question. On April 12, 1945,
President Roosevelt unexpectedly died. Vice President
Harry S. Truman was immediately sworn in as president.
What would this change in administration mean for the
Manhattan Project?

Chapter 4

DROPPING THE BOMB

"The lightning has struck. The lightning has struck!"
President Truman said this was his first, frantic
thought when he learned of Roosevelt's death. Within an
hour, Vice President Truman became President Truman.
Within the next 24 hours, the new president experienced
another emotional and mental jolt. For the first time, he
heard all about the secret Manhattan Project. He discovered
that even though the atom bomb had yet to be tested, the
military had begun training to use it. The training focused
on bombing Japan.

In September 1944, Lieutenant Colonel Paul W. Tibbets
Jr. had been given command of a new Army Air Forces
group. This veteran pilot led the 509th Composite Group as
they practiced flying the new B-29 bomber. It was the only
plane big enough to carry an atom bomb, which would be
larger and heavier than regular bombs. It would also have a
different shape. Tibbets and his men had practiced dropping
loads of concrete the weight of an atom bomb. They also

Harry S. Truman had served as vice president for only 82 days before he became president.

dropped "pumpkin bombs." These were filled with ordinary explosives but shaped like an atomic bomb. Tibbets' group flew at the altitudes and speeds they would use over Japan.

President Truman also learned that there was enormous controversy about using an atom bomb. Was it right to employ such a destructive weapon? It would kill countless civilians as well as enemy soldiers. What would be the consequences of unleashing such destruction? One scientist at Los Alamos, Joseph Rotblat, had already left the project, in December 1944. Because the war in Europe was winding down, Rotblat believed it was immoral to continue work on the bomb.

Scientists throughout the project had meetings about these issues. The controversy grew after Hitler's forces surrendered on May 8, 1945. With the war in Europe over, the threat of a Nazi atomic bomb no longer existed. On June 11, a group of scientists, including physicists Glenn Seaborg and Leo Szilard, summed up their concerns in the Franck Report (named for its chief author, James Franck).

Joseph Rotblat, who left the Manhattan Project in 1944, later won the Nobel Peace Prize for his work to prevent nuclear war.

The Franck Report advised against attacking Japan with an atom bomb. Instead it suggested demonstrating the power of the bomb in an uninhabited area. Its authors predicted that a nuclear arms race would begin if the United States used an atomic weapon. In part the report said:

> *Nuclear bombs cannot possibly remain a "secret weapon," at the exclusive disposal of this country, for more than a few years. The scientific facts on which their construction is based are well known to scientists of other countries. Unless*

an effective international control of nuclear explosives is instituted, a race of nuclear armaments is certain to ensue following the first revelation of our possession of nuclear weapons to the world. Within ten years other countries may have nuclear bombs. … We believe that these considerations make the use of nuclear bombs for an early, unannounced attack on Japan unadvisable. If the United States would be the first to release this new means of … destruction upon mankind, she would sacrifice public support throughout the world, precipitate the race of armaments, and prejudice the possibility of reaching an international agreement on the future use of such weapons. Much more favorable conditions for the eventual achievement of such an agreement could be created if nuclear bombs were first revealed to the world by a demonstration in an appropriately selected uninhabited area.

Scientists at Los Alamos, however, still excitedly awaited the results of Operation Trinity on July 16. Ground zero for the blast was 210 miles (336 km) south, in a desert area near Alamogordo, New Mexico, known as Jornado del Muerto (Spanish for "Dead Man's Walk"). Would their long, hard work produce an atomic explosion? Had they solved the problems of detonating the plutonium inside the test bomb? How large would the blast be?

The staging area for the first atomic bomb test was in an area of the desert known as Dead Man's Walk.

Observers bet among themselves about the size of the blast. A few wondered whether they would survive the explosion. Some people even bet that the bomb would set Earth's entire atmosphere on fire. Reporter William Lawrence was among the observers. He had filed three articles to cover three possible outcomes. One reported a harmless ammunition explosion, while another mentioned injuries. The third article reported the deaths of the observers.

Located 10 to 25 miles (16 to 40 km) away from ground zero, some observers prepared for the blast by lying face down on the ground. Others put on special glasses to shield their eyes and looked toward the test site. The heavy atom bomb was atop a steel tower 100 feet (31 meters) high, its sturdy columns sunk 20 feet (6 m) below the surface. After Operation Trinity's bomb exploded at 5:29 that morning, almost nothing remained of the tower. The heat and force of the blast had turned its steel into vapor.

President Truman immediately received news of the success. He had already decided to use an atom bomb—if it worked—against Japan. Using this terrible weapon would

The Operation Trinity explosion vaporized the large steel tower that had held the atomic bomb.

prevent hundreds of thousands of casualties—the number of killed and wounded troops that military leaders thought a traditional attack on Japan would cost. They had described such an attack, code-named Operation Downfall, to the president.

Military and political advisers had also pointed out other possible consequences of Operation Downfall. Lengthy battles in Japan could give the Soviet Union time to extend its power in Europe and Asia. The Soviet Union was an ally during the war, but the United States disagreed with its communist ideals. The Manhattan Project's secrecy was aimed at possible communist spies as well as Nazi ones. Truman told British leaders about the success of Operation Trinity, but he did not give specific information to Soviet leader Joseph Stalin. Truman said only that the United States had "a powerful new weapon."

On July 17—one day after the Trinity test explosion—155 Manhattan Project scientists signed a petition to the president. They asked him to use "restraint" with atomic weapons. They urged him to consider "the moral responsibilities involved" with this awful weapon. Yet General Groves delayed the delivery of the petition so that Truman did not receive it for several months—long after the weapons had been used. It is doubtful that the petition would have changed the president's mind. Thrust into the presidency without international experience, he relied heavily on official advisers.

On July 26, 1945, along with other Allied leaders meeting in Potsdam, Germany, Truman called upon Japan to surrender. Their Potsdam Declaration warned Japan that the "alternative" was "prompt and utter destruction." It was the only warning that would be given.

The Japanese were not told what would happen to them if they did not surrender. The atom bomb was not demonstrated in order to show them what would happen. They did not know the kind of "utter destruction" that was on its way toward them. When Japan did not surrender by July 29, Colonel Tibbets' group was ordered to "deliver its first special bomb as soon as weather will permit," and they were told that additional bombs were to follow.

There were four possible targets. Few Americans had heard of them. The whole world, though, would soon know the names of two of these cities: Hiroshima and Nagasaki.

Colonel Paul W. Tibbets Jr. and crew

Chapter 5

HIROSHIMA AND NAGASAKI

arly on August 6, 1945, Colonel Tibbets and his 11-man crew flew into history. Their B-29 bomber left Tinian Island in the western Pacific Ocean headed toward Japan, with the words *Enola Gay* painted boldly on its side. This was Tibbets' mother's name. He wanted to honor her as he set out on this vital mission. Tibbets had been told this raid would shorten the war by six months.

The *Enola Gay* carried the atom bomb known as Little Boy. Containing uranium, Little Boy was 10.5 feet (3.2 m) long, 29 inches (74 centimeters) in diameter, and weighed 9,700 pounds

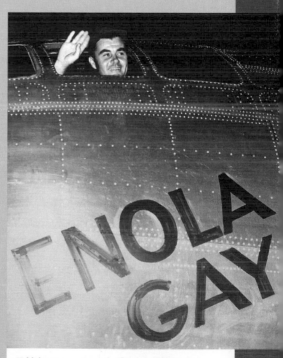

Tibbets waved from the cockpit before takeoff on August 6, 1945.

THE STORY OF THE **ATOMIC BOMB**

(4,400 kilograms). One of the crew said it looked like "an elongated trash can with fins." Tibbets and his men did not know their final target until they were under way. They learned then that good weather had made Hiroshima the best target among the selected cities. Each city contained some military supplies or soldiers, but none had been damaged by traditional bombs. It would be easy to judge the effects of an atom bomb on such locations.

A clear, sunny sky brought destruction to Hiroshima. At 8:16 A.M. Hiroshima time, Little Boy exploded 1,900 feet (580 m) above the courtyard of Shima Hospital. Its blast was equal to 12,500 tons (11,340 metric tons) of the high explo-

An atomic bomb of the Little Boy type

sive TNT. The temperature at ground zero was 5,400 degrees
Fahrenheit (2,982 degrees Celsius). Immediately 70,000
of the city's 76,000 buildings were destroyed or damaged.
Instantly 110,000 civilians and 20,000 soldiers died. Thousands died from injuries during the next few weeks. Death
claimed more than half of Hiroshima's population. Listing
these facts, though, does not communicate fully the horror of
the atomic blast. The words of survivors do.

A young woman who was in Hiroshima recalled seeing

A scene of near-total devastation two miles (3.2 km)
from where the atomic bomb exploded over Hiroshima

"people who had been burned to reddish-black and whose entire bodies were frightfully swollen. Making their way among them are three high school girls … [whose] faces and everything were completely burned and they held out their arms in front of their chests like kangaroos with only their hands pointed downward: from their whole bodies something like thin paper is dangling—it is their peeled-off skin which

A young survivor helped his badly burned brother in the aftermath of the Hiroshima bombing.

hangs there. ... [T]hey stagger exactly like sleepwalkers."

By that night, a 14-year-old boy could hear people "crying and groaning with pain and begging for water." One person "was so burned that we couldn't tell if it was a man or a woman. The sky was red with flames. It was burning as if scorching heaven." A fifth-grade girl heard "moans that penetrate to the marrow of your bones and make your hair stand on end." She said, "I do not know how many times I called begging that they would cut off my burned arms and legs." A fourth-grade boy watched his mother die over the next few days. The hole in her chest grew larger, her moans grew weaker, and then she did not recognize him. He said that "too much sorrow makes me like a stranger to myself, and yet despite my grief I cannot cry."

Some U.S. officials expected Japan to surrender after this terrible attack. They did not realize, though, how Hiroshima's destruction would hinder communication. It was more than a day before details of the blast began reaching Japan's leaders. There was little time left to debate surrender before the U.S. ordered its second atomic attack.

On August 9, 1945, a B-29 bomber piloted by Major Charles W. Sweeney dropped the plutonium bomb called Fat Man over Nagasaki. Seventy thousand people were immediately killed in this port city, where the torpedoes that blasted ships in Pearl Harbor had been built. As in

"IT'S ATOMIC BOMBS"

Official U.S. press releases and newspapers revealed the Manhattan Project's success on August 6, 1945. "IT'S ATOMIC BOMBS" was the front-page headline in one newspaper. President Truman called the project and the bombing of Hiroshima "the greatest achievement of organized science in history."

On August 12, 1945, the government issued a longer official report, titled *Atomic Energy for Military Purposes*. Written by physicist Henry DeWolf Smyth (and sometimes called the Smyth Report), this document explained the science and engineering behind the bombs. It was another year before U.S. citizens learned about the human costs of the bombings.

John Hersey's moving account of six Hiroshima survivors appeared in *The New Yorker* magazine in August 1946. Published as a book titled *Hiroshima*, Hersey's powerful work has remained in print ever since. Reporter George Weller was not as fortunate. His eyewitness account of Nagasaki soon after its bombing—including descriptions of radiation poisoning—was censored by the U.S. military. *First Into Nagasaki* did not appear in print until 2006.

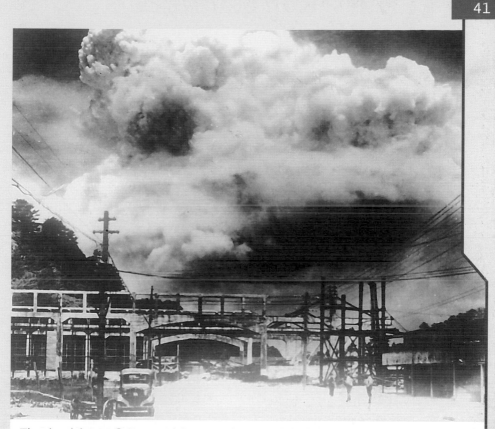

The bombing of Nagasaki was photographed by a Japanese citizen.

Hiroshima, ghastly scenes of destruction were everywhere. And as in Hiroshima, within days people mysteriously began to sicken or die from radiation poisoning. Until then this illness had been almost unknown. Over the next five years, about 140,000 more people in Nagasaki alone would die from radiation-caused illness.

The two atom bombs achieved the results that U.S. leaders wanted. On August 15, 1945, Emperor Hirohito of Japan announced Japan's surrender. Over the radio, he told his people that "the enemy has begun to employ a new and

Like Hiroshima, Nagasaki lay completely in ruins after the dropping of the atomic bomb.

most cruel bomb, the power of which to do damage is indeed incalculable, taking the toll of many innocent lives. ... This is the reason why We have ordered the acceptance of [their terms of surrender]."

The war was over. In the United States and other Allied countries, people cheered and celebrated. Some cried with relief. Yet another war—a different, colder kind of war— was about to begin. And this new war would bring the threat of atom bombs 4,000 times as strong as the ones dropped on Japan.

"THANK GOD FOR THE ATOM BOMB"

Historian Paul Fussell was a young U.S. Army lieutenant during World War II, and his unit was scheduled to invade Japan. Fussell later described the relief soldiers felt when the plan changed. He wrote:

Thank God for the atom bomb. ... [N]ot just a staggering number of Americans would have been killed in the invasion. Thousands of British troops would have been destroyed too. ... When the atom bombs were dropped and news began to circulate that ... in a few months we would not be obliged to rush up the beaches near Tokyo assault-firing while being machine-gunned, mortared, and shelled, ... we broke down and cried with relief and joy. We were going to live. We were going to grow to adulthood after all. The killing was all going to be over, and peace was actually going to be the state of things.

─□ Chapter 6

THE COLD WAR

A tomic power! It was both exciting and dreadful to think about this awesome force in 1940s America. Popular magazines wildly predicted that atomic power would soon cook food, run cars, and heat homes. Radios played tunes such as "Atomic Cocktail," and kids mailed away cereal box tops to get "atomic" rings or gadgets. Yet the only real atomic devices being made were weapons.

At the newly formed United Nations, the Soviet Union in 1946 refused to sign an agreement limiting atomic weapons. The arms race predicted by the Franck Report had begun.

In fact U.S. production of atom bombs had not stopped after Japan's surrender. Although the Atomic Energy Commission, created in 1946 (now renamed and part of the Department of Energy), put civilians in charge of nuclear research, the military continued to demand—and receive—more bombs. In 1946 the U.S. Navy tested the effects of these weapons on and around Bikini Island in the South Pacific. By 1949 the United States had stockpiled 298 atom bombs.

Between 1946 and 1958, the United States detonated 23 nuclear devices in the area in and around Bikini Island.

When the Soviet Union tested its own atom bomb that year, the so-called Cold War became icy.

This conflict—a war of ideas—had begun at the end of World War II, when the Soviet Union gained control of many countries once held by Germany. In part the Soviets were able to establish communism in Eastern European countries by isolating them. The Soviets would not let people leave, and they kept information and people from entering. British leader Sir Winston Churchill called this rigid control an Iron Curtain. Soon everyone in noncommunist countries was using this term to describe the communist control they feared.

One of these people was physicist Edward Teller. His native country of Hungary was now under Soviet rule. Even during the war, this proud, brilliant refugee believed he could design a more powerful atom bomb. While other scientists at Los Alamos worked on Fat Man and Little Boy, Teller concentrated on planning what he called the "Super." This weapon—later known as the hydrogen bomb, or H-bomb—would have several stages. It would use the explosive force of a chain reaction to trigger the fusion of hydrogen atoms. The resulting thermonuclear blast would be thousands of times as strong as the atomic explosions in New Mexico and Japan.

After the Soviets demonstrated that they had atomic fission weapons, President Truman approved development of Edward Teller's even deadlier bomb. In 1950 Truman

Edward Teller was a strong advocate for the hydrogen bomb.

declared: "It is part of my responsibility as commander in chief of the armed forces to see to it that our country is able to defend itself against any possible aggressor. Accordingly, I have directed the [Atomic Energy Commission] to continue its work on all forms of atomic weapons, including the so-called hydrogen or Super bomb."

Other events also influenced this decision. The United States had recently learned that a Soviet spy, Klaus Fuchs, had been among the Los Alamos scientists. U.S. officials feared that other spies would steal more atomic secrets and place the country in further danger. The hunt for spies and communists became daily news. It led to the famous trial and execution in 1953 of Julius and Ethel Rosenberg. It even led to J. Robert Oppenheimer's being questioned for possible communist beliefs the following year.

U.S. involvement in the United Nations intervention in Korea also shaped Truman's nuclear policy. In the Korean War (1950–1953), the United

The Rosenbergs were the first civilians in U.S. history to be executed for spying.

JUDGING JULIUS AND ETHEL ROSENBERG

Ethel Rosenberg's brother David Greenglass was a machinist at Los Alamos. He was a communist, and he passed atomic secrets to the Soviet Union. When Greenglass was captured in 1950, he pleaded guilty to espionage and offered information in order to reduce his prison sentence. He told the FBI that his sister and her husband, Julius Rosenberg, had helped him. The Rosenbergs declared that they were innocent. They and their young sons were often in the news. Greenglass was sentenced to 15 years in prison. The Rosenbergs, however, were sentenced to death. The judge at their trial in 1951 addressed the Rosenbergs:

> I consider your crime worse than murder ... [where] the criminal kills only his victim. ... I believe your conduct in putting into the hands of the Russians the A-bomb years before our best scientists predicted Russia would perfect the bomb has already caused, in my opinion, the Communist aggression in Korea, with the resultant casualties exceeding 50,000 and who knows but that millions of more innocent people may pay the price of your treason.

In 2008 a confession revealed that although Julius Rosenberg was a spy, Ethel Rosenberg probably was not. People had lied about what she did. This makes her final letter to her 6- and 10-year-old sons particularly moving. On the day in 1953 that she was executed, Ethel Rosenberg wrote: "We wish we might have had the tremendous joy ... of living our lives out with you. ... We press you close and kiss you with all our strength. Lovingly, Daddy and Mommy."

States supported South Korea in its fight against communist North Korea. The might of communist China and the Soviet Union shadowed this conflict. General Douglas MacArthur, commander of U.N. forces, asked for and received the "go-ahead" to use atom bombs in the war if the enemy used them first. Fortunately this did not occur.

If an atom bomb had been used in Korea, unequaled human disaster would have resulted. In 1952, when the United States tested its first hydrogen bomb in the Marshall Islands, the entire island of Elugelab was destroyed. Only a huge crater remained. The blast was 500 times as powerful as the bomb that exploded at Nagasaki. In 1953 the Soviet Union continued the nuclear arms race by detonating its first test H-bomb. (In 1952 U.S. ally Great Britain had also become a nuclear power, detonating a plutonium bomb similar to Nagasaki's Fat Man.)

When President Dwight D. Eisenhower declared in 1955 that "A-bombs can be used … as you would a bullet," his false belief reflected U.S. policies and opinions. Fallout shelters, it was said, would keep people safe from atomic attacks and radiation. Through the Civil Defense program, the government built public fallout shelters. Some families built private shelters in their homes. Schoolchildren were taught to "duck and cover" during an atomic attack. They practiced this drill in schoolrooms, using their desks for shelter.

Families hoped to find safety in the event of nuclear attack in fallout shelters, such as the premade Kidde Kokoon.

The false sense of security that was created, though, covered up some doubts. These were apparent in movies that featured monsters created by atomic radiation. In the movie *Them!* giant ants attacked people, while in *The Beginning of the End*, radioactive vegetables turned locusts into gigantic monsters. In *The Incredible Shrinking Man*, a radioactive cloud shrank a man until he became too tiny to see. These horror films were meant to thrill viewers, but other events forced Americans to confront the real horrors of nuclear warfare.

In 1955, 25 victims of the Hiroshima blast arrived in the United States for plastic surgery. The scars and suffering of these "Hiroshima Maidens"—seen in newspapers and on television—showed Americans some of the actual results of atomic warfare. That year scientists and others united to protest nuclear war. At an international peace conference in Pugwash, Nova Scotia, in Can-

Godzilla, the famous movie monster from the 1950s, has a nuclear backstory: Ilis powers are a result of atomic radiation.

ada, the philosopher Bertrand Russell and Albert Einstein spoke out. They urged "peaceful means for the settlement of all disputes ... since nuclear weapons threaten the existence of mankind." Scientist Joseph Rotblat, who had left the Manhattan Project before the Trinity blast, was one of the leaders of the group. In a related effort, the United Nations in 1957 began supporting peaceful uses of atomic energy through the International Atomic Energy Agency.

In the next few decades, protests against nuclear arms took place around the world. Scientists pointed out that a nuclear winter—with soot from explosions blocking sunlight and lowering temperatures—might face the survivors

A nuclear missile waited in its silo

of atomic warfare. Still the stockpiles of atom bombs grew. Engineers built missiles that could carry atomic weapons to distant targets.

In October 1962, people waited breathlessly to see whether atomic war would break out between the United States and the Soviet Union. The United States had discovered Soviet atomic missiles in Cuba, just 90 miles (144 km) away from Florida. The situation was called the Cuban missile crisis. After a tension-filled week, the Soviet Union withdrew the missiles.

Over the next few decades, the United States and the Soviet Union reached a series of agreements limiting nuclear tests and weapons. They included the Partial Test Ban Treaty of 1963, the Nuclear Non-Proliferation Treaty of 1968, the Anti-Ballistic Missile Treaty of 1972, the Intermediate-Range Nuclear Forces Treaty of 1987, and the Strategic Arms Reduction Treaty of 1991. The treaties pushed back the hands of the symbolic "Doomsday

In 1987 Soviet President Mikhail Gorbachev and U.S. President Ronald Reagan signed a treaty to destroy 1,750 nuclear missiles.

Clock" imagined by atomic scientists, which counts down the time to "catastrophic destruction." Yet during the same period, other countries developed their own atomic weapons. France (in 1960), China (in 1964), and India (in 1974) tested atom bombs. Their scientific achievements meant that the Cold War was no longer the only one that might lead to nuclear disaster. Now regional conflicts could also flare into atomic blasts.

In 1991 the Soviet Union collapsed into separate countries. The Cold War was over, but the story of the atom bomb continued.

Chapter 7

NUCLEAR NIGHTMARES AND DREAMS

The decision to drop the atom bomb on Japan has remained controversial. In 1995 the Smithsonian Institution in Washington, D.C., had a special exhibit titled "The Crossroads: The End of World War II, the Atomic Bomb, and the Cold War." The exhibit, at the National Air and Space Museum, featured the restored *Enola Gay*. Veterans, however, protested the exhibit's descriptions and photos of bombed Hiroshima and Nagasaki. They felt that the exhibit showed too little respect for the lives and contributions of the U.S. military. After the Smithsonian changed the exhibit to please the protesters, questions arose again about whether dropping the bombs had been really necessary.

The year 1995 highlighted nuclear nightmares and dreams in other ways. Scientist Joseph Rotblat won the year's Nobel Peace Prize for his efforts in the international Pugwash Conferences against nuclear war. In addition a worldwide children's peace organization was created in honor of Sadako Sasaki, a young girl who survived Hiro-

Protesters outside the National Air and Space Museum argued that the *Enola Gay* is a destructive symbol that should not be displayed in a museum honoring human achievement.

shima's atomic blast. Before she died at age 12, Sadako had folded more than 1,000 paper cranes, the Japanese symbols of peace. Her story is known around the world. Statues of Sadako stand in Seattle's Peace Park as well as in Japan's Hiroshima Peace Memorial Park.

Around the globe, the atom bomb has captured the imagination of artists. In Japan, cartoonist Keiji Nakasawa was a 6-year-old in Hiroshima when the bomb fell. His manga series *Barefoot Gen* (begun in 1973) describes life during and after that atomic blast. It has been made into an animated film and TV series and has been translated into English. The 1989 Japanese movie *Black Rain* looks at the lives of

Hiroshima residents immediately after the bombing and five years later. Famous Japanese film director Akira Kurosawa's 1991 film *Rhapsody in August* shows the effects of the Nagasaki bombing on one family.

In the United States, composer John Adams created an opera about the Manhattan Project in 2005. Titled *Dr. Atomic*, it explores the thoughts and emotions of the people who built the first atom bomb. In 2007 an American documentary film about the bombings in Japan was nominated for an Academy Award. *White Light, Black Rain: The Destruction of Hiroshima and Nagasaki* contains interviews with survivors and modern Japanese teens.

Fascination with the atom bomb continues, in part, because atomic weapons are an ongoing and increasing threat. In 1998 Pakistan acquired the atom bomb. In 2003 the United States invaded Iraq because it was believed that Iraq was hiding "weapons of mass destruction," including atomic bombs. (No such weapons were found.) North Korea became a nuclear power in 2006. Israel and Iran are other countries that already have or soon will have nuclear weapons.

The theft and illegal sale of radioactive materials make it possible for terrorists to build and transport small nuclear weapons. This means that a nuclear attack could take place without any national declarations of war. Even the peaceful uses of nuclear power plants to generate electricity bring their

Since 2006, North Korea has conducted nuclear and missile tests while refusing to engage in international discussion about its nuclear program and ambitions.

own dangers. They create radioactive waste and might have nightmarelike accidents, giving off dangerous radiation. A minor accident at Pennsylvania's Three Mile Island nuclear power plant in 1979 frightened many people. A major accident at Chernobyl in Ukraine in 1986 caused deaths and massive evacuation. For all these reasons, President Barack Obama in his 2009 inaugural address pledged to "work tirelessly to lessen the nuclear threat" facing our planet.

The next chapters in the story of the atom bomb have yet to be written. Whether they will tell of violence or peace remains to be seen.

Timeline

☐ **1938** German scientists produce nuclear fission

☐ **1939** Albert Einstein writes a letter about atomic weapons to President Franklin D. Roosevelt; World War II begins in Europe

☐ **June 1942** Roosevelt authorizes the Manhattan Project

☐ **December 1942** The first successful atomic chain reaction is produced

☐ **April 15, 1943** Work on an atomic bomb begins at Los Alamos, New Mexico

☐ **April 12, 1945** President Roosevelt dies; President Harry S. Truman learns of the Manhattan Project

☐ **July 16, 1945** An atomic bomb is successfully tested at the Trinity site in New Mexico

☐ **August 6, 1945** Little Boy is dropped on Hiroshima

☐ **August 9, 1945** Fat Man is dropped on Nagasaki

☐ **1946** The United States tests an atomic bomb on Bikini Island; John Hersey's article "Hiroshima" is published; the Atomic Energy Commission is formed

☐ **1949** The Soviet Union tests an atomic bomb; the arms race begins

☐ **1952** The United States tests its first hydrogen bomb; Britain tests its first atomic bomb

1953 The Soviet Union tests its first hydrogen bomb;
Ethel and Julius Rosenberg are executed

1955 Hiroshima Maidens visit the United States; the Hiroshima
Peace Museum and Peace Park is dedicated; *Peace Manifesto*,
by Bertrand Russell and Albert Einstein, is published

1957 The United Nations begins supporting peace efforts
through the International Atomic Energy Agency

1962 The Cuban missile crisis brings the United States
and the Soviet Union to the brink of war

1964 China becomes a nuclear power

1968 The Nuclear Non-Proliferation Treaty is signed

1974 India tests its first atomic bomb

1991 The Cold War ends with the breakup of
the Soviet Union

1995 Smithsonian museum hosts controversial exhibit;
Joseph Rotblat receives the Nobel Peace Prize;
a children's worldwide peace organization is created

1998 Pakistan becomes a nuclear power

2003 The United States invades Iraq, suspecting that it has
"weapons of mass destruction"

2006 North Korea becomes a nuclear power

January 20, 2009 President Barack Obama mentions removing
the "nuclear threat" in his inaugural speech

Glossary

chancellor	title of the highest elected leader in some countries
communist	person who believes in an economic system in which goods and property are owned by the government and shared in common; personal freedoms are often limited
electrons	negatively charged particles that are usually found in the outer layers of an atom
fission	splitting of an atom's nucleus into smaller parts; in heavy elements, such as uranium and plutonium, the splitting releases energy
fusion	nuclear reaction in which small nuclei combine to form bigger ones, releasing energy in the process
hydroelectric power	electricity produced using the mechanical energy of moving water
magazine	storehouse for weapons and ammunition
nuclear	related to the nucleus, the positively charged dense core of an atom
nuclear reactor	device that starts and controls a chain reaction in order to use the energy released in the reaction
nuclear winter	drop in global temperature predicted as a result of atomic war
nucleus	positively charged dense core of an atom
plutonium	radioactive, metallic element created in nuclear reactors
pyrotechnics	fireworks for fun or as a result of the explosion of weapons or ammunition
radiation	microscopic particles given off by unstable atoms and various nuclear materials
thermonuclear	related to atomic weapons based on the fusion (rather than fission) of atoms
uranium	radioactive metal; heaviest element that occurs in nature

Additional Resources

Investigate Further

Feynman, Richard P. *Surely You're Joking, Mr. Feynman!*
New York: W.W. Norton, 1997.

Hersey, John. *Hiroshima*. New York: Vintage, 1989.

Klages, Ellen. *The Green Glass Sea*. New York: Viking, 2006.

Klages, Ellen. *White Sands, Red Menace*. New York: Viking, 2007.

Langley, Andrew. *Hiroshima and Nagasaki: Fire From the Sky*.
Minneapolis: Compass Point Books, 2006.

Lawton, Clive. *Hiroshima: The Story of the First Atom Bomb*.
Cambridge, Mass.: Candlewick Press, 2004.

Ottaviani, Jim, et al. *Fallout: J. Robert Oppenheimer, Leo Szilard,
and the Political Science of the Atomic Bomb*. Ann Arbor, Mich.:
General Tektronics, 2001.

Sullivan, Edward T. *The Ultimate Weapon: The Race to Develop the
Atomic Bomb*. New York: Holiday House, 2007.

Weller, George. *First Into Nagasaki: The Censored Eyewitness
Dispatches on Post-Atomic Japan and Its Prisoners of War*.
New York: Crown Publishers, 2006.

Internet Sites

FactHound offers a safe, fun way to find Internet sites
related to this book. All of the sites on FactHound have
been researched by our staff.

Here's all you do:

Visit *www.facthound.com*

FactHound will fetch the best sites for you!

Select Bibliography

Conant, Jennet. *109 East Palace: Robert Oppenheimer and the Secret City of Los Alamos*. New York: Simon & Schuster, 2005.

Fermi, Rachel, and Esther Samra. *Picturing the Bomb: Photographs From the Secret World of the Manhattan Project*. New York: Harry N. Abrams, 1995.

Kelly, Cynthia C., ed. *The Manhattan Project: The Birth of the Atomic Bomb in the Words of Its Creators, Eyewitnesses, and Historians*. New York: Black Dog & Leventhal Publishers, 2007.

Harwit, Martin. *An Exhibit Denied: Lobbying the History of* Enola Gay. New York: Springer-Verlag, 1996.

Rhodes, Richard. *Dark Sun: The Making of the Hydrogen Bomb*. New York: Simon & Schuster, 1995.

Rhodes, Richard. *The Making of the Atomic Bomb*. New York: Simon & Schuster, 1986.

Szasz, Ferenc Morton. *The Day the Sun Rose Twice: The Story of the Trinity Site Nuclear Explosion, July 16, 1945*. Albuquerque: University of New Mexico Press, 1984.

About the Author

Natalie M. Rosinsky is an award-winning author of more than 100 books, articles, and activities for children and teens. Three of her books focus on the Vietnam War era: *The Draft Lottery*, *The Kent State Shootings*, and *The Vietnam Veterans Memorial*. As a schoolchild in the 1950s, Natalie was taught to "duck and cover" during an atomic attack. That is just one reason she believes in questioning authorities and doing thorough research.

Index

Index